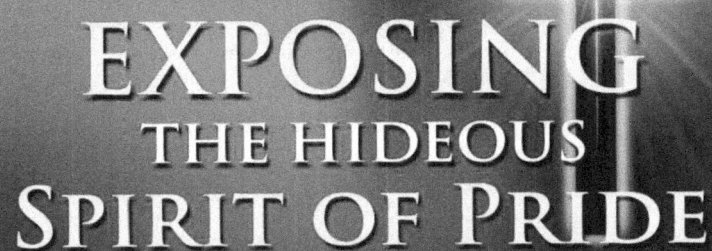

EXPOSING
THE HIDEOUS
SPIRIT OF PRIDE

A Spirit of Deceit, and Humilitty

DOROTHY HARRIS FISHER

Books to Hook
PUBLISHING

DEDICATION

I dedicate this book to all of God's people and all believers in Christ. It is with urgency, high priority, and deep respect that I write this book. The spirit of pride has taken a stronghold on God's people and is at the forefront of most churches today; therefore, it must be confronted and properly addressed. God is reforming His church back to its original place in Him. He is raising those who will help educate His people about the truth of His Word before the return of His Son to the earth. If the spirit of pride is not dealt with, the lives of many will be destroyed by it. Again, it is with honor that I dedicate this book to each of you.

ACKNOWLEDGMENTS

First and foremost, I give honor to my heavenly Father, Jesus the Christ, who instilled into me the words to write this book. I give special thanks to my beloved, fireball, and sister, Dr. Evangelist Tamike Brown, who has a great zeal for the Lord and has encouraged and motivated me with the zeal to write this book. I also give special thanks to my best friend, my dearest, beloved husband, Earnest Fisher, who through his patience and loving-kindness, encouraged and supported me every step of the way from writing, editing, and rewriting to the completion of the book. And last, in respect and honor, I thank God for my dear beloved late grandmother, Maggie Odom, who instilled in me her wisdom, and support, and helped rear me into the woman that I am today. Without the Lord and all of you, it would not have been possible to write this book. Thank you!

TABLE OF CONTENTS

"My people are destroyed for lack of knowledge…"
(Hosea 4:6)

Today, you shall know the truth, "and the truth shall make you free." (John 8:32)

FOREWORD
Evangelist Earnest Fisher

This is a must-read book, especially for every born-again believer. The author lays bare the hideous and deceptive spirit of pride, which has destroyed the lives of many good people. The author writes this book with easy understanding so you can identify with areas in your life that may be prideful. After reading this book, I am encouraged that you will be strengthened and enlightened to defeat the spirit of pride and live a victorious life.

CHAPTER 1

PRIDE AS A PART OF MAN FALLEN NATURE

Being prideful is a part of our fallen nature as human beings, whether we want it to be or not. It was pride that led to our first parents, Adam and Eve's downfall as they ate the forbidden fruit in the garden of Eden. In this, they were cursed and fell from their original state of being immortal to being mortal, knowing good and evil. And the curse fell upon all of us, and thus in iniquity were we all conceived (Psalm 51:5).

The spirit of pride is evil and cruel as cancer. It slowly steals, kills and destroys. It begins its destruction as mild and entertaining; being cute and funny. We see the evidence of its deadly manifestation early in the lives of our children.

According to the Bible, pride is a haughty spirit (Proverbs 16:18). It is to be puffed up, high-minded, conceited, or lifted up in oneself and one's ability and strength. Pride also lifts oneself above others including God. It is an evil spirit (demon). The spirit of pride is seen in everyday society, yet its presence seems to go unnoticed. This could be because mankind has become accustomed to its presence and the fact that it's second nature to us.

The spirit of pride is also seen in the church of God, and it has brought great disaster to many individuals, families, communities, nations, and the world at large.

God hates pride. He considers it as an abomination unto Him because the spirit of pride loves to exalt itself as God and it leads to one's destruction. Friend, it is dangerous to be prideful and see yourself as equal to God because you will fall into His hands of judgment. Ask Lucifer, the light-bringer, who was kicked out of heaven and sentenced to eternal damnation, as he thought in his heart that he would be like the Most High (Isaiah 14:14). Only God is God, and no one else is to be seen or put as His equal.

Pride comes before one's fall or destruction (Proverbs 16:18). The spirit of pride gives you an inflated ego with a false sense of security and belief in yourself. The spirit of pride elevates and exalts you above others manifesting in thoughts such as I am better than others, smarter than others, more skillful than others, prettier and sexier than others, and so forth. And whenever you exalt yourself above others, you have put yourself in the same position as God because only God, and not mankind, is to be exalted above others.

The spirit of pride has been perpetuated by the American dream, which is to pursue fame, wealth, popularity, power, beauty, honor, worship, and to be all that you can be and all that you want to be. The spirit of pride is universal as it affects all races, and different races of people come to America to pursue the American dream which is to be idolized and be your own god.

God tells us in His Word that His people are destroyed from a lack of knowledge (Hosea 4:6). Therefore, it is the purpose of this book, and by the grace of God, to help expose the enemy's lies and the deceitful spirit of pride that destroys many. It is the little foxes that spoil the whole flock, so the truth shall be revealed that the people may be free.

As stated earlier, God hates pride and does not take its seriousness lightly. Similarly, we should also hate the spirit of pride and not take its seriousness lightly. We must remove it from our lives as it can lead to eternal damnation.

CHAPTER 2

THE HIDEOUS AND DECEITFUL SPIRIT OF PRIDE

The spirit of pride is hideous and deceitful. It promises you greatness, yet it slowly and cunningly destroys you and leads to your downfall. It tries to hide behind you if you are a renowned person or stand in a position of authority in influencing others' behaviors. Your standing positions of authority can range from low to high, from a job team leader to the president of a nation, from a father in the home to a pastor in a church, or from a home caretaker to a schoolteacher.

The spirit of pride solemnly covers itself up by having you put on a false air in front of others, portraying yourself to be more than you actually are. You may even go as far as putting others to shame to make yourself look good.

The spirit of pride is hideous and deceitful because it will have you believe that you have the wisdom and power to know and fix everything and everybody. It loves to take control, and sometimes, it can be seen in marital and family relationships. You, the spouse, who is usually the wife, subconsciously or consciously, may believe that you are the smarter one in the relationship and try to fix everyone's problems even if you don't know how if you were asked to. Your husband, on the other hand, expects you to listen only and not play the role of God of knowing and fixing everything. Though you as the wife may see yourself as being helpful, in reality, this is considered a sign of dishonor and disrespect to your husband. Your reactions imply to your husband that he is not intelligent enough to resolve his own problems. However, if given the opportunity, your husband may well be capable of resolving his problems but just not in the manner in which you, the wife, would expect him to.

Interestingly enough, you are playing the role of God by taking control and wanting to fix everything. The bible warns us against trying to be like God. Rather you are to allow your mind to be at rest, pray and seek God concerning His perspectives on everything. The Word of God says that you (us) are to consult God first in everything and He shall direct your paths, by imparting His wisdom to fix your problems (Proverbs 3:5-6).

The spirit of pride is hideous and deceitful because it darkens your consciousness, leaving you unable to recognize the spirit of pride in your own life and even in your home, church, school, or community. This is mainly because the spirit of pride is a part of man's fallen nature and you have become accustomed to it being a part of your normal upbringing. The spirit of pride may even go unrecognized as the root cause of relationship and business failures, divorces, family discords, hate crimes, church divisions, and so forth.

The spirit of pride is hideous and deceitful in that it will shamefully force you to be timid and shy, unknowingly allowing others to control your soul and mind in exchange for praise and acceptance from them. You may enjoy having your flesh tickled while living in fear of how others perceive you. You may even lower yourself to be humiliated by others in exchange for favor or promotional offer, such as a job promotion.

The spirit of pride is hideous and deceitful because the truth concerning its origin has been concealed through lies and deception throughout generations. This has been a crafty plan of the enemy and you may have fallen victim to these lies. The truth is that Satan, the fallen angel, is the father of pride, as he is the father of all sin and lies.

The spirit of pride is hideous and deceitful because it gradually hardens your heart from receiving from God. It selfishly holds you back from expressing your true God's kind of love in your relationship with Him and others. It also hinders your business relationships and success as the hideous spirit would have you disassociate yourself and prevent you from receiving from others that which could be very beneficial to you. Overall, the spirit of pride robs you from experiencing the true beauty of who you are in the image and likeness of God. In the image and likeness of God, you are a vessel of honor and not dishonor.

The spirit of pride is hideous and deceitful. It can enter and stifle your hearts, preventing you and your spouse from humbling yourselves before each other, an aspect integral to a thriving and prosperous relationship in God. The spirit of pride robs your relationship of its beauty, joy, and dignity, which exist only because you are all made in the image of God the creator.

The spirit of pride is hideous and deceitful, as it cunningly leads you to glorify yourself, your accomplishments, abilities, gifts, and talents. It will also have you glorify your beauty as a god, just as Lucifer did in heaven when he decided that he wanted to be like the Most High (Ezekiel 28:17, Isaiah 14:12-13).

The spirit of pride is hideous and deceitful because it will conceal itself behind jealousy, yet it is a root cause of jealousy, which is also deceitful and destructive to lives and relationships. You may think jealousy is the root cause of one's actions; however, in honesty, pride is likely the root cause of one's actions because jealousy (like anger) stems from pride and often co-occurs with it. It was so with Cain with the killing of his brother Abel as Cain was already prideful in that he did not bring the required sacrificial offering to God. If the root cause behind selfish jealousy in your life is not addressed, you may continue to struggle and find it difficult to overcome the jealousy.

Also, last but not the least, the spirit of pride is hideous and deceitful because it has found its way into the church, which is supposed, to visibly represent God before the world, yet the church itself stands to be reformed by God. More on this subject later.

Chapter 3

RECOGNIZING THE SPIRIT OF PRIDE IN ACTION

The spirit of pride starts in your mind and says, 'I want to be like God, I want to be idolized, worshipped, and looked up to'. This chapter elaborates on some of the things that you may say or do consistently, which could indicate the spirit of pride in play. As you read, you may recognize some of these prideful things in your own life, allowing you to address and overcome them.

For instance, If you regularly engage in conversations with others and say things such as, 'I know, I know,' or 'No, I got it, I don't need any help, I can do it myself,' you're likely to have the spirit of pride controlling your conversations and actions. You may also passively believe that you know everything. If someone points out the spirit of pride in your life, you usually refuse to believe it. You may be the one that has an answer for everything. You may even tend to debate with others as your pride will not allow you to be wrong, even if you are in error.

Gaining knowledge may inflate your ego. You may love to show off your knowledge, whether speaking publicly before others or not, as you love to hear others say that you are smart, which keeps you puffed up. You may enjoy 'reaching out for more and more knowledge' to the point where you may believe that you know everything and may even giggle about it. However, your quest for knowledge outside of God is a downfall. You shall eventually be led to that dark path where there is no more knowledge to gain. Your knowledge as a person is limited and comes to an end because you are not equal to God. The bible lets us (you) know that you are to consult God for wisdom and understanding in everything you do.

If you, on purpose and regularly, mentally shut off people with the pretense of listening and receiving from them during conversations, you are likely being controlled by the spirit of pride in your life.

If you are a person who persistently refuses others' help or to even ask for help when you know that you need it, you are likely to have the spirit of pride controlling your life. In this instance, you usually resort to solving the problem on your own, even if it means working overtime, before swallowing your pride to accept or ask for help.

If you are easily upset when someone asks you a simple question, corrects you, or gives you constructive criticism, you are likely to have the false god of pride controlling your actions. You may not appreciate having your wisdom or judgment in question, even in response to simple statements such as 'please repeat what you just said'. Also, you may not want to be wrong in whatever you say or do. You may repeat the same task over and over again to make sure everything is perfectly right, even if it was correct the first time. You may do this to avoid receiving confrontation and rebuke from others, especially from those in positions of authority.

If you find yourself easily offended by other people's actions, such as road rage, or someone purposefully hanging up the phone as you are talking to them, then the spirit of pride may be influencing your life. The spirit of pride stirs in you and says, 'I dare you to insult my intelligence and hang up the phone on me. Who do you think you are to hang up the phone on me? I am better than you.'

As mentioned earlier, if you despise authority or persistently get mad and roll your eyes in retaliation when being confronted with instructions or directives from those in authority or leadership, you are likely being controlled by the spirit of pride in your life. For instance, despite being capable and well-trained, you may get mad and roll your eyes in response to your job supervisor's gentle directive asking you to work today in another department due to high demand. You become puffed up in response and may quietly say to yourself such things as, "No one tells me what to do, I am the one to instruct them, they are no better than me, but I am better than them." However, the Bible instructs and commands us to humbly submit ourselves to others and not to be rebellious and stubborn to each other.

If you persistently hate to humble yourself and admit to yourself or to others when you are wrong concerning anything, you are likely being influenced by the spirit of pride in your life. You may subconsciously believe that you are perfect and could never do any wrong or that you are too good to do such a menial task of lowering yourself before others and admitting your wrongs.

If you are a person who easily and persistently gets offended or angry with every misfortune or bad thing that happens to you, your loved ones, or friends, your life is likely being controlled by the demon (evil) of pride in you. You may see yourself as being too good and above others (with whom your compare yourself) for bad things such as sickness, death, or job loss, to happen to you or your loved ones.

If you see yourself as being better than others, your life is likely being controlled by the demon of pride. You may dislike people and avoid interacting with them as you believe that you are better than them. For example, you may be an expert in using a software application but reluctant to help the new employee to learn it because you are too puffed up, don't like people, and are unwilling to humble yourself to help the new employee.

You may also see yourself as being better than those who hurt you in your past. If so, your focus in life is usually on yourself and your past. You may find it difficult to advance in life, as the spirit of pride in you keeps you dwelling on yourself and your past. You may also retaliate and look down on your enemies as you see yourself above them. You may walk around angry and prideful. Jonah of the Old Testament was such a person. Jonah was very angry with God for relenting his judgment against the people of Nineveh. Perhaps Jonah did not like the Ninevites due to their harsh treatment of them as the children of Israel.

If you are a person who persistently rebels or hardens your heart against God and His Will for your life, you are likely to have the demon of pride operating in your life. You intentionally refuse to obey God's commandments and rather choose to follow the imaginations of your own evil heart of doing your own thing. For instance, God may repeatedly tell you to forgive someone, but instead of humbling yourself to do so, you consistently harden your heart and refuse to forgive. One reason for this is that the spirit of pride may puff you up to see yourself as being too good to stoop low to someone whom you deem not worthy of the honor of forgiveness.

If you are nosy just for the sake of wanting to know everything, you are likely to have the demon of pride controlling your life and actions. You may be in a room where three conversations are going on at the same time, and you try to listen to all the three conversations at the same time. The spirit of pride would have you wanting to know everything and about everybody. This role is for God, and only God has this capability.

If you are a person who regularly entertains imaginations of having your ego flickered, of being popular, rich, or famous, or who loves to be looked upon by others as someone great or important, you are likely to have the demon of pride influencing your life. You may enjoy the thrill of having others be dependent upon you to satisfy your flesh for praises and to be looked upon as a god. If you are a person in a position of authority, such as a pastor, governor, teacher, counselor, singer, name them, you are likely prone to these thoughts of pride. However, you need not be in some position of authority or leadership to be influenced by the spirit of pride in this area of your life.

If you persistently boast arrogantly and talk proudly of your talents, abilities, or accomplishments, you are likely being influenced by the spirit of pride in your life. You may tend to be snooty, walk around with your chin and heads up in the air, and purposefully bypassing others without any form of acknowledgment.

If you are a person who sees yourself as better than or above others in different areas of maturity, you are likely being controlled by the spirit of pride in your life. You may measure your righteousness against the righteousness of others instead of the Word of God. You may regularly condemn and judge people in their relationships with others, their talents, abilities, their decision-makings and wisdom, and so forth. You may say things such as, 'how can he be so evil and wicked when he's supposed to be a church goer', or 'how can she bypass and not speak to me when she is supposed to be a praying woman of God', or 'how can he say he loves God and still lives in sin.' You may find yourself proudly rejoicing in others' failures as you are puffed up in yourself (Obadiah 1:13).

If you are a person who regularly says or does things to make others look small so that you may look good in the eyes of others, you are likely being influenced by the god of pride in your life. For instance, your motive is to impress Joe X that you are very knowledgeable and spiritual. You do this by telling Joe X that you counseled Tom X on how to forgive and get his life right with God. As a result of your actions, you now hope that you have gained Joe X's respect so he may honor you and see you as a knowledgeable and spiritual person to consult with in the future if needed.

CHAPTER 4

LESSONS TO LEARN FROM BIBLICAL PEOPLE WITH PRIDE

The bible teaches us to guard our hearts with all diligence (Proverbs 4:23), but from my personal observation, we do not do so all too often. The word 'guard' means to give due diligence by staying alert and watchful. Just as a security guard is always alert and watching to guard a city or a building from intruders, we too, especially believers of Christ, are always to guard our hearts against the spirit of pride's intrusion.

The bible tells us that pride happens in the heart before a fall (Proverbs 16:18), and throughout the bible, we have examples of mighty men who fell due to the spirit of pride operating in their lives. It is wise to take note of and learn from these biblical characters so that you may avoid the same pitfalls in your life.

In the bible, we learn that King Nebuchadnezzar experienced a mental illness and was isolated for seven years because of his prideful heart. The king became prideful after he conquered many surrounding nations and gained great honor. He believed that it was his own power and strength that got him his fame, honor, and royal residence as Babylon the Great. Daniel 4:30 (ASV) says of the king, "Is not this great Babylon, which I have built for the royal dwelling-place, by the might of my power and for the glory of my majesty?". Here, the king was wrong in his thinking for the bible states that every good and perfect gift comes from the Father above. God is the one who empowered King Nebuchadnezzar and gave him his glory, yet the King failed to humble himself and acknowledge God as the source of his power, glory, and honor.

The spirit of pride crept into king Nebuchadnezzar's heart. Even after God had warned the king several times through dreams to humble himself and repent, the king, in all his folly, still refused to humble himself, repent, and acknowledge God as the source of his power and glory. The king appeared to enjoy the glory, attention, and honor that came with his conquering power, even going so far as saying, "I am a god."

As the king refused to humble himself from his prideful ways, he was stripped of his royal crown and fell from his rulership for seven years. King Nebuchadnezzar was driven away from people (into the wilderness) and he ate grass like an ox. His body was drenched with the dew of heaven until his hair grew like the feathers of an eagle and his nails like the claws of a bird. The king had the smell and the mind of a wild animal for seven years until he came to himself.

In other words, the king had experienced a mental breakdown. He lost his right mind. And one interesting thing about king Nebuchadnezzar is that he was aware of his current state of condition, that his right mind had been replaced by that of an animal. The king was humiliated as he was brought low. It was after the seven years in fulfillment of the prophecy that King Nebuchadnezzar humbled himself, and he was given back his right mind and his kingdom was restored. For the bible says,

And at the end of the days I Nebuchadnezzar lifted up mine eyes unto heaven, and mine understanding returned unto me, and I blessed the most High, and I praised and honoured him that liveth forever, whose dominion is an everlasting dominion, and his kingdom is from generation to generation: and all the inhabitants of the earth are reputed as nothing: and he doeth according to his will in the army of heaven, and among the inhabitants of the earth: and none can stay his hand, or say unto him, What doest thou? At the same time my reason returned unto me; and for the glory of my kingdom, mine honour and brightness returned unto me; and my counsellors and my lords sought unto me; and I was established in my kingdom, and excellent majesty was added unto me. Now I Nebuchadnezzar praise and extol and honour the King of heaven, all whose works are truth, and his ways judgment: and those that walk in pride he is able to abase. (Daniel 4:34-37)

The lesson to be learned from King Nebuchadnezzar of Babylon is that whenever God or someone God uses points out pride in your life, be mindful to humble yourself, examine your heart, and repent before God. Carefully guard your heart against perceiving yourself to be someone of great stature when you have gained power, position, honor, and wealth in life.

Another biblical character to learn from is king Rehoboam, who was young and a novice in his leadership role as King of Israel. King Rehoboam took the advice of his young friends, as opposed to the advice of the wise elders in the land, when it came to the northern tribe's request to lessen the hardship that was put upon them by his father, King Solomon. If King Rehoboam lessened the burden, the northern tribes would have served him as king of Israel. However, the king made the wrong choice by making the northern tribe's workload even harder than that which his Father Solomon had imposed upon them. The king's downfall from his unwise decision resulted in a revolt among the people of Israel, and his kingdom being split into two, the northern and southern kingdoms. The lesson to be learned from King Rehoboam is that as a beginner in a new role or position, you should not assume that your position or role comes with wisdom or that you know it all. Wisdom comes when you revere the Lord and maintain a teachable spirit with a willingness to learn from others. Never be arrogant and perceive in your heart that 'you know it all', whether you are a newlywed spouse or novice in your role or position. It is imperative for you to stay in close communion with God and those who are seasoned and close to the heart of God.

King Agrippa is another person in the Bible who had a prideful heart and was struck with sickness. His downfall resulted from his acceptance of the people's worship in the claim that he had the voice of a god after he had given a great speech. However, the king should have given God the glory and directed the people to do the same. Since the King failed to do so, he had a downfall in his health. As a part of God's judgment, he was consumed with worms and died (Acts 12:23). The lesson from this is that you are to carefully guard your heart against the temptation of secretly receiving the people's praise and worship, especially after a great deed or performance. For instance, you may lay hands on a sick person, and the person immediately heals. You may also speak with words of wisdom or deliver a profound speech that would astound your entire audience. Such acts may attract others, who may see you as a god and worship you. They may look at you in amazement or say things such as 'you are an angel (god), you are so awesome.' And as a person of influence, you diligently have to guard your heart against becoming prideful or being lifted up as a god through the praises of others. People may not see what goes on in your heart, but God always knows and sees it.

One way to guard your heart against this type of King Agrippa's pride is to quickly correct those who may see you as a god. Instruct them to give the glory to God as you do the same. In doing so, you keep yourself humble, and the people are likely to appreciate you and less likely to see you or any other leader as their crux or god, which is idolatry. Only God alone is to be exalted and worshipped on this high level and not a mere man.

Lucifer is another biblical character who became prideful and fell from heaven with a lesson to be learned from him. Lucifer was one of the original sons of God, the light-bringer in heaven, and he is still a real spiritual evil being today. Lucifer was an angel of beauty and splendor, the seal of perfection. His downfall was that he allowed his beauty and splendor to corrupt him. He was so prideful in these things that he imagined himself to be like the Most High, and he was cast out of heaven. For the Word of God says,

Thine heart was lifted up because of thy beauty, thou hast corrupted thy wisdom by reason of thy brightness: I will cast thee to the ground, I will lay thee before kings, that they may behold thee. (Ezekiel 28: 17 KJV)

The lesson to learn is that you are to appreciate the beauty and the glory that God gave unto you. However, you are to guard your heart against becoming overzealous with your beauty. If you do not guard your heart, as it was with Lucifer, you begin to see yourself as a god or goddess, worship yourself, and desire for others to do the same toward you. However, the Bible forewarns us that in the last days, people shall become lovers and worshippers of themselves (2 Timothy 3:2).

The Word of God also clearly states that (you or we) are not to think more highly of yourself than you ought, but to think of yourself according to the measure of faith that God has assigned to each person (Romans 12:3). The Bible also warns you not to get caught up on your outer appearance of beauty, particularly women, who should adorn themselves in modesty with decent and appropriate clothing that will not draw attention to themselves by the way they fix their hair, wear golds, pearls and expensive clothes (1 Timothy

2:9). Adorning yourself in modesty shows your true beauty in the way God created you to be while maintaining a humble spirit before God and others.

Another lesson to learn about pride is from the biblical parable of the rich young ruler. In Luke 12:13-21, the Bible tells us that the rich young ruler looked around at the many goods that he had accumulated and decided in his heart that he would build bigger barns to store all of his goods. But God answered him and said in verse 20, 'Fool! This night your soul will be required of you; then whose will those things be which you have provided?' The rich young ruler had a vain show in what he had accumulated. Psalm 39:6 states, "surely every man walketh in a vain shew: surely they are disquieted in vain: he heapeth up riches, and knoweth not who shall gather them."

The rich young ruler was proud in his heart of the many goods that he had accumulated for himself. It was as though he would be set for life with no need to worry about anything. However, he failed to acknowledge and honor God as the source of his many goods, and God required of his soul to die.

The lesson to be learned from the rich young ruler is that you are to avoid putting on a vain show, privately or publicly, with the goods which God blessed you with. Everything on the earth belongs to the Lord, even cattle on a thousand hills belong to the Lord. Therefore, it is arrogant for you to believe that you are the real owner of your goods. You are only a steward over God's goods; thus, you are to stay humble and be thankful for the goods that God entrusted in your care. You are also not to be selfish and think that the goods are only for yourself, but for others. Throughout life, you must be careful not to allow material goods cause you to become vain and conceited as though 'you have it going on.' It is imperative that you acknowledge and reverence God for all that he empowers you to get, whether it is a house, a car, fine clothing, education, wisdom, degrees, and so forth.

Pharaoh, in the book of Exodus, is another biblical figure to learn from regarding the spirit of pride. Pharaoh's heart was hard against God in that he refused to obey God and insisted on doing things his way. God had warned Pharaoh several times to let his people go so that they may go and worship Him in the wilderness, but Pharaoh kept resisting. Pharaoh trusted in his mere man's wisdom and power, and God had to prove to Pharaoh that he was no match to Him as the Almighty God. God sent ten plagues, with the last plague killing the first-born son in every Egyptian family. It was after then that Pharaoh's heart softened to let God's people go. Yet, in all of this, Pharaoh did not acknowledge God as the ultimate power. Pharoah continued to trust in his mere man's wisdom and strength, believing that he could outdo God by having his army chase after the Israelites after he had let them go. However, Pharaoh's plan did not succeed as his army was drowned in the Red Sea. The lesson to learn is if you don't humble yourself, then God will. You are not to rebel against God and allow your heart to become prideful to the point where God Himself has to humble you. You are to stay submissive and walk humbly before the Lord. It is possible that if Pharaoh had humbled himself before God, perhaps he would have avoided the consequences of the plagues. Yet in all of Pharaoh's rebellion, God still loved him.

Lastly, we are to learn a lesson about pride from the children of Israel, who were God's own personal possession among all the nations of the earth. God promised them all the promises of Abraham if they kept His commandments. Wow, What a blessing! Yet, prideful Israel did not obey God, but they continued to murmur, complain, and stubbornly rebel against God. Prideful Israel didn't trust in God's wisdom or His way of doing things. Rather, they chose to be their own god by following the evil imaginations of their own hearts. They trusted in their own strength and considered themselves well-capable of making decisions and choosing what was best for them. They didn't need God's help as long as things were going well for them. Is this not the classic spirit of pride that we witness in our own lives and world today? (Exodus 16:2-7, Numbers 14:2, 27, Jeremiah 13).

"Pride! Pride! Pride!" It was pride that led to the Israelites' downfall of them being taken away from their land. The god of pride deceived the children of Israel to believe that they were their own god and that they could do what God could do. They couldn't, however, make manna rain down from heaven or water come from a rock. Even after being rebellious, God still loved backsliding Israel and would to this day that no nations or persons on earth look down in disgust upon Israel, His chosen people. God repeatedly had to humble His people until they came to their senses and acknowledged Him as their only God and served Him alone. The lesson to learn is that you have to diligently guard your heart against murmuring and complaining as these are signs of a rebellious and prideful heart, and God hates a prideful heart. You ought to always obey God and depend upon Him instead of living from the counsel and imagination of your heart, which God says is evil. It is important to remember that God is the source of life and all blessings. And when you obey God, you will be unto Him for a people, and for a name, and for a praise, and for a glory (Jeremiah 13:11).

CHAPTER 5

BOWING DOWN UNAWARE TO THE GOD OF PRIDE

Behind every evil spirit is a false god or what we may also call a fallen angel in play. Many are unaware that the god of pride is controlling their actions. Every time you yield to the evil spirit or temptation of pride, you bow down to the false god or the fallen angel of pride, giving credence to its power in your life.

Many people, including those in the body of Christ, unknowingly, have and continue to bow down to the false god of pride. You may think that you are the one influencing your own evil actions, believing that you are just a mean, hateful, and wicked person. However, it is not you who controls your actions, but the false god of pride, a real spiritual being that is in you. And if this false god of pride is not addressed and dealt with on time, it will eventually lead to your downfall. It may also destroy your marriage, family, church, and even your community.

In general, our understanding of the spirit of pride, the fallen angels, and the false gods is limited due to a lack of knowledge and in-depth teaching on the topic. Even our basic understanding of what is a false god or fallen angel has been twisted by the enemy for the purpose of keeping you and all people blind to its true identity.

As such, you may have fallen victim to the spirit of pride. You may have been deceived to believe that the spirit of pride is not a real being and is not associated with one of the false gods or fallen angels from heaven. You may have been taught that the fallen angels or false gods are just another fairy tale that took place in the ancient world. You may believe that it is a force, power, or wind with no significance or life.

Just because spiritual beings can't be seen with the natural eyes, it does not mean that they are not real beings or do not exist. These spiritual beings are just as real as you and I.
They can move, speak, and see just like human beings. The only difference is these beings do not possess a terrestrial (earthly) body, but they have a celestial (heavenly) body. As the Bible makes mention of the fallen angels as being real, you should also believe that these spiritual beings (fallen angels) are real, and these fallen spiritual beings or angels are still present in our world today.

The enemy has rampantly used this information of misconception of his nature and origin as a weapon to keep you divided and in disarray with people including those in the house of God.

As it remains, there has been far too little true teaching on the spirit or the false god of pride. The church is guilty of not sharing the truth with the people. God's Word says that His people are destroyed for a lack of knowledge (Hosea 4:6), and people lack knowledge because the truth is kept from them. And the end result is that people's lives are short-changed, existing beneath the privileges that God created them to have.

As the spirit of pride runs rampant in the universe, you along with others may not recognize its signs and symptoms in your life, making it difficult for you to address this spirit within yourself. The spirit of pride can even lie dormant without the knowledge of your natural senses until it has corrupted your life and your relationship with other people including those in your families, communities, and churches. Your good plans may have been destroyed or never brought into reality because the god of pride was at work unknowingly in your life.

As a believer in Christ for many years, I have noticed particularly in the church world that the term "fallen angel or god" or "the fallen angel or god of pride" are rarely used. Perhaps one reason for its rare use is to avoid instilling intimidation and fear in the lives of the people. It is less frightening and easier to say the 'spirit of pride' versus 'the fallen angel or the god of pride" which may instill fear that a living being is present.

The enemy has done a good job in behooving the church to believe his lies in order to keep God's people in bondage to the spirit of pride. Howbeit, the god of pride has to be thoroughly addressed and taught truthfully by God's appointed leaders if the people are to overcome and conquer this demon or false god of pride in their lives.

The Word of God specifically commands that we are not to bow down to any other deity besides the Almighty God (Exodus 20:3). The spirit of pride is a false deity. And as stated earlier, each time you give in to the temptation of pride, you have worshipped or bowed down to the false deity (god) of pride, and have committed sin. However, God is merciful to forgive you of your sins, and when the truth of God's Word has been presented to you, God expects you to repent from your sins and serve Him.

So make the conscious decision today. Choose to bow down and serve the Almighty God, and not the false god of this world system; do not yield to the spirit of pride. Be watchful and guard your heart with all diligence against the spirit of pride. For at the end of the day, you shall give an account to God for your life choices and deeds.

CHAPTER 6

BEING CHURCHY YET DIVIDED BY A SPIRIT OF DECEIT

It is a wonder how God practically allowed nearly all businesses and churches around the world to close down during the Covid-19 pandemic of 2020. It was a downtime for the churches including the body of Christ, to do a thorough examination of itself, and to re-evaluate what spirit has actually been in the headship of its church and its services. As with others, Christianity has become another religion that is driven by church programs and money-making schemes to support itself as a business versus as a house of prayer. Christ Jesus is not head of the church, but Satan is, as sin predominates the church from the pulpit to the pews, just as it was in the Old Testament with the Israelites in the house of God.

A large portion of church services today is prideful in and of themselves. The prayers, faith confessions, praise and worship services, and believers' interactions with each other are prideful. We say that we love the Lord, but we talk down to and belittle each other. Is this not churchy or what? The Bible tells us that as children of God, each of us is to please his neighbor for his good, which leads to edification or a building up (Romans 15:2).

However, within ourselves, we frown and look down in disgust at one another. We tend to make ourselves look good at the expense of others. Is this not churchy or what? The Word of God says in Romans 14:10 "But why do you judge your brother? Or why do you show contempt for your brother? For we shall all stand before the judgment seat of Christ." And Romans 15:1 says, "We then that are strong ought to bear the infirmities of the weak, and not to please ourselves."

We (you) disrespect and avoid showing dignity to all for the selfish reason of thinking that we (you) are better than others, too important to stoop low to those to whom we compare ourselves. Is this not churchy or what? God created all of his creatures in His image and likeness, and the Word of God commands that we are to have respect for all persons, which includes all creed, race, nationality, economic status, and social or living conditions.

In arrogancy and out of disagreement, we question God's judgment or wisdom on a matter, as though we know what is best and God does not. Is this not churchy or what?

Our church prayers and personal prayer times and relationship with God have become prideful. We pray to God as though He owes us something, not knowing that this type of posture before God is arrogancy. We give God a commandment as though He has to do something for us or else He is not God. In arrogancy, we say, 'God if you don't do this, then I won't do this, 'I won't serve You any longer, I will stop serving on the deacon board, I will quit going to church, I will quit preaching, I will quit telling people that you are good.'

The sad thing is that many, and you may be one of them, have come to believe that their behaviors and posture before God are acts of faith towards Him and that God is pleased. The enemy has deceived us by the spirit of pride. In reality, God is not pleased when we approach Him in this type of posture of arrogance. If we (you) carefully think about it, we shall come to realize that we cannot command or make God do anything for us, but we can only humbly ask or petition the Father for his help. God commands and expects us to humble ourselves before Him instead of being prideful and rebellious.

God wants us to wake up and come to our senses and realize that we are on the wrong side of the track. In our churches, we have adopted a pretense of faith that we believe is real faith because we have been acting churchy for so long.

However, being churchy is pride. It is religion at its best. It is being piously while covering oneself with the name of Jesus. Being churchy does not please God and it has to stop before the wrath of God descends on the earth.

CHAPTER 7

MY PERSONALTESTIMONY
A Near Mental Breakdown Experience

In January of 2019, I began my journey to having a renewed mind in Christ, free of the spirit of pride. Before then, I had been attending church faithfully for many years, but I was hell-bound because I did not have the mind of Christ. For 10-12 years, the Lord tugged at my heart for me to have the mind of Christ as it is written in Philippians 2:5-8, "Let this mind (or personality) be in you, which was also in Christ Jesus." I didn't know what all of that meant and didn't respond properly to the Holy Spirit's promptings.

Let this mind be in you, which was also in
Christ Jesus: who, being in the form of God,
thought it not robbery to be equal with God:
but made himself of no reputation, and took
upon him the form of a servant, and was
made in the likeness of men: and being found
in fashion as a man, he humbled himself, and
became obedient unto death, even the death
of the cross. (Philippians 2:5-8 KJV)

As I paused, thinking back to the year 2000, God had revealed to me that a spirit of pride had attached itself to my life. As it was minimal, I ignored it and thought (out of ignorance) that it was rather cute to have a little pride in me. Therefore, I didn't address it at all. Little did I know of its seriousness and the devastating effect that would come later on.

Returning to telling my story, in the prior year of 2018, I began to hear clearly within my inner self that a spirit of jealousy was trying to attach itself to my life. I examined my heart, but I was unable to find who or what I was jealous of. And as time went by, I began to hear the Holy Spirit's promptings in my heart stronger and stronger regarding the spirit of jealousy trying to attach itself to my life. I couldn't help but wonder if it was my jealousy or a jealous spirit I felt towards me.

I did not realize how serious the spirit of jealousy was until it attacked me one day, pronouncing evil thoughts in my mind for me to repeat and carry out. Immediately, I knew that was not the right thing for me to say, do, or feel as the spirit was not from God. I pulled and cast down that evil spirit and thoughts from my mind right away. If I had ignorantly acted upon those evil thoughts and words, that deceitful spirit of jealousy would have entered my heart and taken control, ruining my life, destiny, and future. Not only that, but it would have ruined my relationships with those who were important to me: my husband, my sister, my family, and friends, or anyone who may have stood in opposition to me.

Not knowing exactly where this evil spirit came from or why it was trying to attach itself to my life, I began to search my heart, meditate on God's Word, and ask the Holy Spirit to show me my error(s). I did not want the spirit of jealousy to enter and rule my heart and take control of my life. I repeatedly asked God to remove that spirit of jealousy from me before it entered my heart, but God later let it be known that the pride in my heart had to be broken.

The spirit of pride was the root cause behind my attacks and behavior. It was also so with Cain in Genesis 4:1-7, with a little of jealousy. Cain, perhaps like many of us, was not in tune with his prideful, fallen nature, which loves to be glorified and exalted above others. The spirit of pride was already at work in Cain's life as he did not bring to God the firstlings of the required offering as his brother Abel did. Perhaps, Cain thought he was smarter than God by bringing Him less than the required offering. Or perhaps, he thought 'God didn't really mean what He said' or 'he could impress God with something better than the firstlings.' Whatever Cain's reason was, God did not have respect unto him and his offering as He did with Abel. And as a result, Cain was very angry and had a fallen countenance. God asked Cain "why are you angry (not jealous) and why do had a fallen countenance? And if you do the right thing, shall not you be respected?". God told Cain that if he didn't do the right thing, sin was lying at the door. And from reading the Word, it appeared that Cain had the opportunity to humble himself, repent, correct his rebellious self and do the right thing but he did not. Instead, his sin gave way to him slewing his brother after he had talked to him. And when God inquired of his brother's whereabouts, Cain responded to God and said, 'I don't know. Am I my brother's keeper?' You see, it was more of pride instead of jealousy behind Cain's sin and the killing of his brother.

Howbeit, since the spirit of pride is so cunning, it may not be so obvious and easily recognizable as the spirit of jealousy. It is not good to be ignorant of the spirit of pride, which is a spirit of deceit. It is also not good to be ignorant of the spirit of jealousy, as it is also a spirit of deceit. The enemy uses your ignorance against you to destroy you for his evil pleasure and purpose.

Returning again to my story, in the year 2018, as time went by, I began to pay closer attention to my personal life and drew closer to God and His Word. The Holy Spirit began to remove the scales from my eyes, revealing to me the hidden evilness behind the jealous spirit that the enemy planned to use against me, which came from a prideful and hardened heart. I actually saw in the spirit realm demonic activities in action to carry out their evil plan against me, and boy, this did not make the devil happy; my heart had become enlightened to the craftiness and truth of his evil plans. The enemy got madder and became more aggressive in his attacks against me, to defeat me and take over my mind. …But greater is he that is in you, than he that is in the world (1 John 4:4). God was on my side!

It is amazing how the enemy tries to do his evil work when you take the least notice; when you are vulnerable, such as when you are sick, or when you are asleep in bed. That is how the enemy works, cunningly. The enemy knows that if he comes straight at you and not sneakily, he will be caught red-handed and defeated on the spot.

As stated earlier, the enemy was not through with me; he became stronger and more aggressive in his attacks against me, especially during my sleep time.

One special night in 2019, as I lay partially asleep in bed, I had a tugging at my body, tapping on my legs and feet, to get up and pray. (I realized later that they were the angels of the Lord). However, I ignored the tugging and tapping on my body because I wanted to sleep. I wasn't aware that the enemy had devised a plan to take away my mind that night, but the Holy Spirit was aware. That is why I was beckoned to get up and pray, but I declined and turned over in bed to finish sleeping.

As I continued to lie partially asleep in bed that night, all of a sudden, just as it was with Adam and Eve in the Garden of Eden in Genesis 3:7 when their eyes became open (to evil), a quick change took place in my heart, and my eyes became open in the spirit realm. I saw darkness and demonic activities taking place in my mind. And as the demonic spirits saw that I took notice of them, they stood up and fought speedily against my mind to quickly gain control of it.

I was left in the dark and I was totally lost to myself as to what to do next. I looked inside the walls of my heart for answers, only to find out that it was empty and dark. I became very nervous and frightened by what was happening to me. I tried to understand, but there was nothing for me to understand, reason, or know because it was as if I already knew everything in eternity, that I needed to know and understand. That may sound odd, but it was true; there was nothing left in eternity for me to grasp, or at least that's how I felt in my state of mind due to the spirit of pride. I came to understand that knowledge ran out because there is no more knowledge at the end road of pride.

Everything was happening so fast. I didn't know how to prevent what was happening to me. I was scared and cried out softly to God for help, and behold, I happened to look down by the side of my bed, and saw two angels that were pulling on my arms and beckoning me to get up and follow them. The angels of the Lord helped pull me up and rushed me to the living room, pushing me to the floor on bended knees, and bowing my head and hands to the ground of the earth to worship the Lord. It was in this posture that I began to find comfort, peace, and security in the Lord; not being mentally lost in the fight against the assigned attack of the enemy on my mind.

What a night and experience to remember! I stayed in that posture of worship on bended knees until the break of the day. Afterward, I began to read my bible and meditate on God's Word all into the next day and the days that followed. The Holy Spirit began to teach me how to humble myself and showed me that it was the spirit of pride that had opened the door for the spirit of jealousy to attach itself to my life. The spirit of pride is a spirit of deceit. It wasn't until a few months later that I had some understanding of what took place in my mind and body that night. With the spirit of pride, the enemy was trying to make me snap and have a mental breakdown so that he could take over my life, but God said "no".

I was very shocked at what took place in my life that night, as I considered myself a person of prayer who was always on guard of my heart. But not so, the enemy had devised a plan against me to take away my mind that night. Perhaps because I had gotten to a point in my life where I became very hungry for God and His Word and only wanted to do His Will. The enemy's sole purpose was to stop me from obtaining God's destiny for my life.

From my experience, I learned that it is not only good for you to examine your own heart, but it is also wise to ask God to search your heart daily to see if there is anything wicked in it. The enemy wants to take your mind so that he may control it. If he takes your mind, the enemy knows that you are a defeated foe. And then the enemy and his army of demons will sit back and laugh, saying, "she is crazy, haven't you heard that she has lost her mind and she supposed to be holy?"

I can only imagine the mental or nervous breakdown that people go through. It is a very serious and scary experience for them. They feel lost in a world of their own with no room for hope. Only God can deliver you from the enemy's attack on your mind for whatever reason.

As stated earlier, the enemy asked to take over my mind, but God said "No." It was there that I began my journey from a prideful spirit to humility, and from an unrenewed mind to a renewed mind in Christ. What a day of rejoicing and victory!

In conclusion, there is an end point to the spirit of pride. When you reach the end point of the prideful spirit that is in your life, there is nothing else for you to hold onto. There is no more understanding to grab onto, no more wisdom to ravish, and no more glory for you to obtain. When the spirit of pride (a false god) enters your heart and controls your life, you are left to fall; you lose the mental control of your life and your faculties are suspended. It is what people call "being crazy or having a nervous or mental breakdown." You are left bowed in a fetal position, crying, trembling, shaking, looking lost and confused because you are at your wit's end. You are in a very dark place because you no longer have control of your understanding of what to do next or where to turn. Someone else has to be your guide, or you are afraid to leave your home, or perhaps you are driven away from your residence as it was the case with King Nebuchadnezzar. The false god of pride robs you of your understanding!

Realize that as a human being, you cannot know everything because you are not the All-Knowing God. In pride, the enemy fools you into thinking you know everything "I know, I know", but you don't know that at the other end of pride is a dark place "where everything you knew you don't know anymore". This is the cunning part of the enemy against you with the spirit of pride. He will cunningly and subtly have you yield to prideful things, slowly and gradually setting you up for the big fall in your life, as he did with Adam and Eve in the garden of Eden. Unfortunately, the enemy doesn't tell you that you will eventually reach the end of your pride and fall off the cliff.

As mentioned earlier in the story of King Nebuchadnezzar, others also have lost their mind to a mental breakdown due to the hideous danger of the spirit of pride. They did not realize that on the other end of the spectrum of pride is "a lost mind that doesn't know what to do". I thank God for His mercy and grace; He did not allow me to have a mental breakdown but He left me to tell my story to help those who may be on the wrong path to pride.

Last, in my thirst for understanding, I asked God, "Why do people lose their minds?" I began to understand from God, that the Holy Spirit always gives warnings, but people often harden their hearts to the continuous promptings of the Holy Spirit. The Holy Spirit will give prompts, such as to renew the mind, to not see yourself as better than others, judge others (which is evil like the sin of adultery), put away jealousy and strife, and love one another as Christ loves you. You may ignore these promptings out of ignorance, and you might take lightly the promptings by the Holy Spirit, denying the seriousness of the issues at hand. However, particularly in our current times, God wants you to seriously take heed of the Holy Spirit's promptings because He sees the big picture that lies ahead of you and knows that the issue at hand will spiral out of control.

The word of God says in Hebrews 3:15, "Today, if you hear my voice, don't harden your hearts as Israel in the desert did when they rebelled." In other words, don't rebel but listen to the Word of God. Whenever the Holy Spirit tugs at your heart, no matter how big or small the situation, stop immediately and address the issue. Take heed of the Holy Spirit's prompting, whether it is to have a renewed mind, be generous, be kind, or whatever. It is for your own good.

I pray by the Word of God that the sharing of my story has touched your heart in some way for the better.

CHAPTER 8

HUMILITY & MEEKNESS

Now that you have been exposed to the truth concerning the hideous and deceitful spirit of pride, you have to make the conscious decision whether you want to be delivered; repent your sins and totally surrender to God. If you are a spouse or a leader and you want this spirit out of your home and church, you have to educate those involved on the truth of pride so that they may repent and humble themselves before God to be delivered from the spirit of pride. Transformation begins when you make the decision to walk in humility and meekness before God.

God's Word says that you are not to think more highly of yourself than you ought. Yet, at the same time, you are not to devalue or look down upon yourself but to think of yourself with sober judgment (Romans 12:3).

In fact, if you are to fulfill the plan and purpose of God for your life, you must, to some degree, according to the measure of faith that God has given to each person, think well of yourself and see yourself as worthy in Jesus.

As you do unto others, you are never to look down upon yourself, but you are to see yourself as God and His Word see you. God created you in His beauty, the image and likeness of Him, and you are to see yourself in this same Beauty. You are to humbly believe that you belong to God and God has crowned you with glory and dignity, as being set apart, chosen, and a royal priesthood unto Him. However, you are not to allow these things that God has said about you to cause you to be conceited or to think more highly of yourself than you ought.

God says in Philippians 2:5-8, let this mind (personality) be in you which was also in Christ Jesus. Jesus was not prideful even though He was one with the Father in having the same attributes and characteristics of the Father. Jesus did not allow the glory that He had in the beginning with the Father to cause Him to be puffed up. He didn't think too highly of himself to be shamefully lowered to the state of a man and became a servant, obedient unto death. Likewise, you should not allow yourself to become high-minded that you are unable to lower yourself in humility to serve God and one another.

Jesus also did not permit his mind to wander and focus on evil thoughts. Neither did He permit His mind to dwell on thoughts that others' opinions of him. Instead, Jesus kept His mind on Father God and the Truth of His Word, and walked in obedience to Him. And Jesus desires the same for us.

One day as it was told to Jesus that he ought to leave town as Herod desired to kill Him, Jesus' response was, 'Go and tell that fox, behold, I cast out demons and perform cures today and tomorrow, and the third day I complete my mission' (Luke 13:32 WEB). In other words, Jesus was not timid, and His heart was not focused on what may be said or done against Him. Jesus had his heart focused on completing His Father's Will and He would not move forward before He completed His three-day assignment in that town.

You should obey the Lord's Will for your life, and to please God, you must walk humbly before Him and others.

To be humble is to be lowly in mind, attitude, and spirit. It is to walk softly before the Lord with a submissive and teachable heart. And as an outward expression of your humbleness and gratitude before God, you may find yourself on bended knees, bowing down before God, the Almighty One, the Creator of the heavens and the earth, giving glory and honor unto Him.

Also, to be humble is an act of your will by the decisions that you make. You make the humbling decision to admit to God and yourself that you do not know everything but only God is the one who knows everything. The Word of God lets us know that anyone who claims to know all the answers really doesn't know what he should know (I Corinthians 8:2).

When you are humble before the Lord, you are conscious of the Lord's presence and give reverence to His Holy Presence, His Kingship, and Lordship in your life.

Besides being humble, you also have to be meek in order to successfully defeat the spirit of pride.

Meekness is having your emotions and strength under control. You are slow to become angry at offenses by others. Your temperance is also controlled when you are put under pressure. In simple terms, to be meek means being cool, calm, and composed under pressure.

God wants you to be meek and humble in mind. God does not want you to have your mind entertain anything that is evil or that is against the mind of Christ. Instead, you are to allow your mind to think on whatever things are true, whatever things are honorable, whatever things are just, whatever things are pure, whatever things are lovely, whatever things are of good report, if there is any virtue and if there is anything worth of praise, "think on these things" (Philippians 4:8). Your thoughts and heart are to be filled with worship, praise, and adoration unto the Lord, by speaking to yourself in psalms and hymns and spiritual songs, singing and making melody in your heart to the Lord (Ephesians 5:19).

You are not to allow your mind to dwell on those things that will cause you to glorify yourself, or to think more highly of yourself than you ought. For instance, you are not to boast about how beautiful you are, how fine in physique you are, how smart you are, how rich you are, as if it was through your own strength or by chance that these things came about in your life. When those thoughts and imaginations come to your mind, you are to cast them down and bring every high thing that exalts itself against the knowledge of God into captivity to the obedience of Christ; (2 Corinthians 10:5). And one way to humble your soul in aligning it with God's Word is through fasting and praying (Psalm 35:13; 69:10-12).

In practicing humility, you also have to bring your body as well as your mind into subjection to the Word of God. Like the Apostle Paul, who disciplined his body and brought it into subjection to God's Word, you, too, ought to do the same (1 Corinthians 9:27).

And if God is to heal you from your past or past hurts, it is imperative that you live a fully surrendered life unto God. You must trust, lean, and solely depend on Him as your deliverer. You have to be teachable and allow the Lord to direct your life's paths and decisions.

If you are prideful and haughty, and you are ready to walk humble and upright before the Lord, you are to humbly repent of your sins before Him, including the sin of pride in your life. You are to live a life of worship in reverential fear before the Lord, and obey His commandments. It is imperative that you meditate on God's Word day and night, and allow God's Word to dwell richly in you in all things. In doing so, you shall not fulfill the lust of the eyes, the lust of the flesh and the pride of life.

And finally, the best way to cultivate humility and meekness in your life is to just practice humbleness and meekness whenever the opportunity presents itself to you. For instance, if someone makes a mistake, instead of looking down and degrading the person, choose to esteem the person more highly than yourself by still showing respect and dignity to the person. Or if someone makes negative remarks or yells at you, know how to contend for the faith without becoming angry and bitter. Practice meekness by not yelling back at the person, but practice with 'silence' or returning a soft answer by saying, 'I am sorry that you are upset. How may I make it right?' Proverbs 15:1 says a soft answer turns away wrath. Remember, humility is not weakness, but it is strength under pressure. Make the decision to be humble and continue to practice humility whenever the opportunity presents itself to you. And if you lack wisdom how to humble yourself, ask God and He shall give you wisdom (James 1:5). And remember God's Word says of you in

Luke 14:11 that whoever exalts himself will be humbled, and he who humbles himself will be exalted.

WORDS OF ENCOURAGEMENT

Revelation 12:11 says, "They overcame by the blood of the Lamb and the words of their testimony." What joyful news to hear! Jesus' blood paid the penalty for our (your) sins. He defeated pride in victory and nailed it to the cross. Be encouraged, you too can defeat the spirit of pride by looking daily unto Jesus as the author and the finisher of your faith in Him. It is only by Jesus' strength (blood), and not your own, that you overcome the spirit of pride. Trust in the Lord with all your heart, lean not on your own understanding, and allow God to direct your path. And as the Lord directs and pinpoints things that are prideful in your life, work on them, as He expects you to because He loves you.

It is also by the word of your testimony in Jesus (the Son of God) that you overcome the spirit of pride. The words of your testimony are Jesus is your healer, savior, and deliverer. Never take your eyes off Jesus, but stay in close communion with the heart of God through prayer, praise, worship, and obedience. Though you shall stumble along the way to your path of victory, never look down on yourself in discouragement. It is just part of the healing process of God developing you into the beautiful you. Instead, be kind to yourself by speaking faith-filled declarations over your life, such as, "I overcome by the blood of the lamb and the words of my testimony. I am healed from pride by the blood of Jesus." Amen!

A PRAYER OF REPENTANCE & DELIVERANCE FROM THE SPIRIT OF PRIDE

Heavenly Father, I humbly bow myself before You in Jesus' Name. I ask You Father to forgive me of my folly (sin) of operating in the spirit of pride and from my stupidity in thinking that I knew what was best for my life. I have sinned, and I pray that you lay not this charge against me.

Lord Jesus, I surrender to You my whole heart, mind, soul, will and spirit. I ask You to teach me Your ways and clothe me in Your spirit of meekness and humility.

Help me not to be prideful and puffed up but help me to be meek and lowly in my mind and in my thoughts.

Lord, I ask You to help me to cast down every high thought and thing that exalt itself against Your Holy

Word and to bring these things into obedience to Christ.

I ask You Lord to help me to practice humility with those I come in contact with and share Your love in my heart with them.

I ask You Lord to help me to acknowledge and revere You, and to consult You in everything I do so that You and not I may receive the glory from my life.

I thank You Lord for hearing and answering Your servant's prayer in delivering me from the spirit of pride of life. For this, I give You the glory in your Son Jesus' Name. Amen.

BIBLE VERSES ON PRIDE & HUMILITY
(King James Version)

Jeremiah 9:23
Thus saith the LORD, Let not the wise man glory in his wisdom, neither let the mighty man glory in his might, let not the rich man glory in his riches:

Proverbs 16:18
Pride goeth before destruction, and an haughty spirit before a fall.

Proverbs 18:12
Before destruction the heart of man is haughty, and before honour is humility.

1 Samuel 2:3
Talk no more so exceeding proudly; let not arrogancy come out of your mouth: for the LORD is a God of knowledge, and by him actions are weighed.

Proverbs 21:24
Proud and haughty scorner is his name, who dealeth in proud wrath.

Proverbs 21:4

An high look, and a proud heart, and the plowing of the wicked, is sin.

Philippians 2:3

Let nothing be done through strife or vainglory; but in lowliness of mind let each esteem other better than themselves.

Proverbs 16:5

Every one that is proud in heart is an abomination to the LORD: though hand join in hand, he shall not be unpunished.

Romans 12:3

For I say, through the grace given unto me, to every man that is among you, not to think of himself more highly than he ought to think; but to think soberly, according as God hath dealt to every man the measure of faith.

Luke 14:11

For whosoever exalteth himself shall be abased; and he that humbleth himself shall be exalted.

Proverbs 27:2

Let another man praise thee, and not thine own mouth; a stranger, and not thine own lips.

Psalm 138:6

Though the LORD be high, yet hath he respect unto the lowly: but the proud he knoweth afar off.

Proverbs 29:23

A man's pride shall bring him low: but honour shall uphold the humble in spirit.

Philippians 2:5-8

Let this mind be in you, which was also in Christ Jesus: Who, being in the form of God, thought it not robbery to be equal with God: But made himself of no reputation, and took upon him the form of a servant, and was made in the likeness of men: And being found in fashion as a man, he humbled himself, and became obedient unto death, even the death of the cross.

Romans 12:16

Be of the same mind one toward another. Mind not high things, but condescend to men of low estate. Be not wise in your own conceits.

1 Corinthians 13:4

Charity suffereth long, and is kind; charity envieth not; charity vaunteth not itself, is not puffed up…

YOUR JOURNEY TO OVERCOMING THE SPIRIT OF PRIDE

After reading this book, I hope you were able to identify specific areas of pride in your life, so you may overcome them and give glory to God. Today, take the time to use this section of the book to write down the things that are prideful in your life, repent of them, and then write down some solutions that will help you overcome them. Some of the prideful things may be obvious and some may not be easy for you to pinpoint. Therefore, I encourage you to start your journey with the Lord by allowing Him to show you the prideful thing in your life. Be teachable and permit others to point out pride in your life. Focus more on God than yourself through prayer, praise, worship, and thanksgiving. And keep practicing humility every time the opportunity presents itself to you. Two examples are provided below to help you begin your journey to defeating the spirit of pride. At the end of your journey, you will like the person that you have become, the beautiful you that God created you to be in Him.

1a. Personal examples of pride in my life:

- ❖ I view myself as better than others.
- ❖ I look down on others.
- ❖ I judge others.
- ❖ I am prejudiced.
- ❖ I am too good to be seen with certain people.

1b. Personal solutions to the pride in my life:

- ❖ Confess: I am meek and lowly in mind.
- ❖ I am not better than others.
- ❖ I have the mind of Christ.
- ❖ I love people. I love to give respect and honor to others.
- ❖ Read & meditate daily on Romans 12:3 & Philippians 2:5-8.

2a. Personal examples of pride in my life:

❖ I know I am smart. I know everything.

❖ I love gaining knowledge; every time, it makes me feel good (puffed up).

❖ I feel good (prideful) when I stand & speak before others.

❖ I love to share my knowledge so others can see how smart I am.

2b. Personal solutions to the pride in my life:

❖ Confess: "Lord, You are the smart one, the God who knows everything. Lord, I know nothing outside of You."

❖ Every day and throughout the day, worship & exalt God on how glorious He is, how worthy He is, etc.

❖ Read & meditate daily on Luke 14:11, Proverbs 2:6, 1 Samuel 2:3.

3a. Personal examples of pride in my life:

3b. Personal solutions to the pride in my life:

4a. Personal examples of pride in my life:

4b. Personal solutions to the pride in my life:

5a. Personal examples of pride in my life:

5b. Personal solutions to the pride in my life:

6a Personal examples of pride in my life:

6b. Personal solutions to the pride in my life:

7a. Personal examples of pride in my life:

7b. Personal solutions to the pride in my life:

8a. Personal examples of pride in my life:

8b. Personal solutions to the pride in my life:

9a. Personal examples of pride in my life:

9b. Personal solutions to the pride in my life:

10a. Personal examples of pride in my life:

10b. Personal solutions to the pride in my life:

ABOUT THE AUTHOR

Dorothy H Fisher is an evangelist and carries a strong prophetic healing anointing. She is also an educator, a healthcare consultant, as well as an inspirational Speaker in the "You Were Meant to Be Happy Series." She works alongside her husband, Earnest Fisher, as co-owner of Dorothy's Healing School of Ministry LLC, located in Middle Georgia. As a first-time author, she writes this book of utmost importance to help those who may be experiencing mental health challenges. This is based on her own experience of a near mental breakdown due to the spirit of pride and her many years of experience as a nurse and nurse practitioner, helping those with mental and physical health challenges.

Dorothy was born and raised in the countryside of Cordele in Southern Georgia by her grandmother Maggie Odom, who is now laid to rest. While growing up, she loved the Lord and attended church faithfully along with her younger and only sister, Tamike Brown. She enjoys worshipping and praising the Lord. At an early age in life, Dorothy realized her calling, to be a speaker of God's Word to millions, and wasn't afraid to make it known amongst her peers during her childhood and high school years. At the age of 18, Dorothy committed her life to the Lord to serve Him, but without error and sin, and she began to grow in God and serve in the church as an usher, teacher, and soul winner. At the age of 39, she was espoused in holy matrimony to a very beautiful, handsome man of God, Earnest L Fisher, her best friend who inspires her a lot to continue to be a lover of God's Word and a lover of God's people.

Dorothy obtained her first ministerial license at the age of 23 doing field and prison ministry. In 2001, Dorothy graduated as a salutatorian and received a certificate of completion at her School of Ministry Class in Macon, Georgia. From there, she continued her journey to teach the Word of God to youth and teenagers, and later to adults in the school of ministry class at her local church of attendance. In 2014, Dorothy got the opportunity to travel out of the country, along with her husband and sister, to do evangelical work in Nigeria and it was there where she was first ordained an evangelist by Bishop Noah at African Global Ministries Network, Int'l, and later again in 2017 at the Covenant Church of Jesus Christ in Macon, GA. In January of 2020, being led by the Holy Spirit, Dorothy's Healing School of Ministry (DHSOM) LLC was established to serve as a healthcare consulting firm that provides holistic healthcare services, whether mentally, physically, or spiritually, to individuals and various organizations.

.

Visit:
www.dorothyhealingschool.com
for more information and other resources